W9-BDH-363

MAY - - 2002

TYRANNOSAURUS REX

A TRUE BOOK

by

Elaine Landau

Children's Press®

A Division of Grolier Publishing

New York London Hong Kong Sydney
Danbury, Connecticut

EAST NORTHPORT PUBLIC LIBRARY
EAST NORTHPORT, NEW YORK

Reading Consultant
Linda Cornwell
Coordinator Of School Quality
And Professional Improvement
Indiana State Teachers Association

Dedication:
For Dr. Lawrence E. Stein—
Miami's greatest dentist!

A model head of
Tyrannosaurus rex

Visit Children's Press® on the Internet at:
http://publishing.grolier.com

Library of Congress Cataloging-in-Publication Data

Landau, Elaine.
 Tyrannosaurus rex / by Elaine Landau.
  p.cm. — (A true book)
 Includes bibliographical references and index.
 Summary: Describes the characteristics and habits
of the massive flesh-eating dinosaur, as well as theories about
why it became extinct.
 ISBN 0-516-20454-8 (lib.bdg.)   0-516-26507-5 (pbk.)
  1. Tyrannosaurus rex—Juvenile literature. [1. Tyrannosaurus rex.
2. Dinosaurs.]   I. Title.   II. Series.
QE862.S3L37   1999
567.912'9 — dc21   98-8277
                                                   CIP
                                                   AC

© 1999 by Children's Press®, a Division of Grolier Publishing Co., Inc.
All rights reserved. Published simultaneously in Canada.
Printed in the United States of America.
 3 4 5 6 7 8 9 0 R 08 07 06 05 04 03 02 01

Contents

Tyrannosaurus rex

Picture a huge dinosaur standing in front of you. It is one of the largest meat eaters ever to walk the Earth. It is ready to attack. As it charges, you see its sharp, curved, knifelike teeth. They line the dinosaur's tremendously powerful jaws. You are about to be eaten by a frightening flesh eater known as *Tyrannosaurus rex*. Fortunately, you will never find yourself in this scary spot. *Tyrannosaurus rex*, along with the rest of the dinosaurs, no longer exists. It lived toward

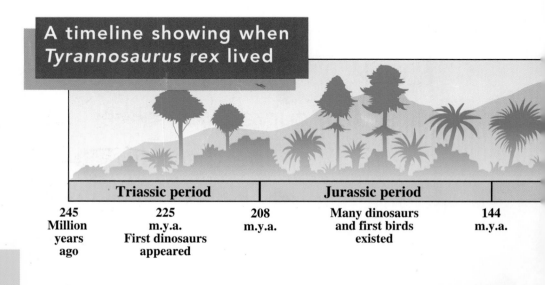

A timeline showing when *Tyrannosaurus rex* lived

	Triassic period		Jurassic period	
245 Million years ago	225 m.y.a. First dinosaurs appeared	208 m.y.a.	Many dinosaurs and first birds existed	144 m.y.a.

the end of the Mesozoic era, a
time also known as the Age of
the Dinosaurs. This era lasted
from about 245 million years
ago to about 65 million years
ago.

Tyrannosaurus rex appeared
during the Cretaceous period,

(Note: "m.y.a." means "million years ago")

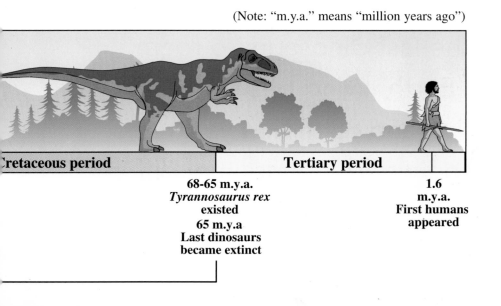

Cretaceous period | Tertiary period

68-65 m.y.a.
Tyrannosaurus rex
existed
65 m.y.a
Last dinosaurs
became extinct

1.6
m.y.a.
First humans
appeared

Tyrannosaurus rex was a meat-eating dinosaur.

the last phase of the Mesozoic era. *Tyrannosaurus rex* was one of the last dinosaurs to roam the Earth, living between 68 million and 65 million years ago.

The world looked very different during the Cretaceous

period. The Earth's continents were still forming. Mountain ranges were just beginning to appear. The dinosaurs of the Cretaceous period were changing as well. Many of the earlier huge, long-necked plant eaters had begun to die out. Now new theropods, or meat eaters, appeared around the globe. These included *Tyrannosaurus rex*, whose name means "king of the tyrant lizards."

A model of *Tyrannosaurus rex*

A Flesh-eating Giant

Of all the dinosaurs, *Tyrannosaurus rex* is probably the best known to young and old alike. It is the ferocious predator often portrayed in movies and books.

Tyrannosaurus rex was a member of a family of massive dinosaurs known as tyrannosaurids. But none are nearly as famous as *Tyrannosaurus rex*.

Tyrannosaurus rex was about 40 feet (12.4 m) long and weighed between 6 and 7 tons. It measured 12 feet (3.7 m) high at its hip—about the height of two fully grown men if one stood on the other's shoulders. When *Tyrannosaurus rex* reared up on its hind legs in a fight, it was about 18 feet (5.5 m) high.

This dinosaur's large head, thick neck, and broad rib cage were balanced by its heavy muscular tail. To achieve this balance, *Tyrannosaurus rex* walked with its tail held stiffly off the ground.

This is how big *Tyrannosaurus rex* would look standing next to a full-grown man.

As this skeleton shows, *Tyrannosaurus rex* walked with its tail held off the ground.

Tyrannosaurus rex's short front limbs were only about as long as human arms. They were neither long enough nor large enough to be helpful in attacking another dinosaur. They also were too short to be used to bring food up to the dinosaur's mouth. So what was the purpose of these small arms?

Tyrannosaurus rex's arms were tiny in comparison to the rest of its body.

This question has long puzzled paleontologists (scientists who study prehistoric life). No one knows for sure, but some paleontologists think that *Tyrannosaurus rex* might have used its arms to prop itself up as it rose from the ground.

When standing, *Tyrannosaurus rex* rested on its large hind legs. These have sometimes been compared to the pillars of a building. The dinosaur's ankles and feet

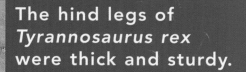

The hind legs of *Tyrannosaurus rex* were thick and sturdy.

were quite large and were shaped like a bird's. Many scientists think that birds actually descended from flesh-eating dinosaurs. The feet of *Tyrannosaurus rex*, like those of a bird, had three clawed

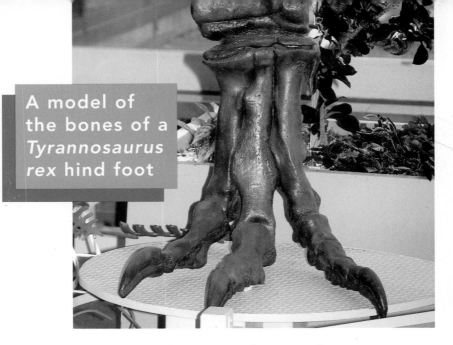

A model of
the bones of a
*Tyrannosaurus
rex* hind foot

toes and one dew claw (a very small, almost useless toe).

Tyrannosaurus rex had a massive, 4-foot- (1.2-m-) long head. Many researchers think that *Tyrannosaurus rex* had fairly good eyesight and hearing. These would have been useful in seeking out prey.

Tyrannosaurus rex probably would have been able to swallow a child in one bite!

The dinosaur's mouth was meant for eating huge chunks of meat. Its lower jaw was hinged. This allowed it to rip off large mouthfuls. *Tyrannosaurus rex*'s teeth were also made for attacking prey. These teeth were up to 9 inches (23 cm) long and sharp as a dagger.

A fossilized *Tyrannosaurus rex* tooth

Tyrannosaurus rex tore apart its meal by gripping the prey with its teeth while swinging its head back and forth. This dinosaur would never have starved to death if some of its teeth fell out. That's because its teeth were constantly being replaced.

Knifelike teeth

The teeth of *Tyrannosaurus rex* have been compared to the blade of a steak knife. That's because like a steak knife, each tooth had serrated edges to cut through flesh more easily. Fossilized *Tyrannosaurus rex* dung has been found containing crushed bone. This means that *Tyrannosaurus rex* was probably able to crush bones before swallowing them!

Fossils

Paleontologists learn about dinosaurs through fossils. Fossils are the remains of animals or plants that have been buried in the Earth's crust for millions of years. The fossils are dug up and pieced together like the parts of a puzzle. The finished products

We know about *Tyrannosaurus rex* through fossils.

give us a picture of the animals that existed on Earth in pre-historic times.

The first somewhat-complete skeleton of *Tyrannosaurus rex* was discovered in northern Montana in 1902. Among the

Tools like these (right) are used to uncover fossils like this *Tyrannosaurus rex* pelvis (above).

fossils uncovered were the dinosaur's jaws and part of its skull. Its hind legs, backbone, shoulders, and mid-section were also dug up. An American paleontologist named Henry Fairchild Osborn was extremely interested in these remains. He studied the fossils, and in 1905, officially named the dinosaur.

In 1908, there was another important finding in the same part of Montana. This time,

The site of a *Tyrannosaurus rex* excavation in South Dakota

paleontologists from the American Museum of Natural History located a nearly complete *Tyrannosaurus rex* skull. Almost a half century later, still other discoveries added

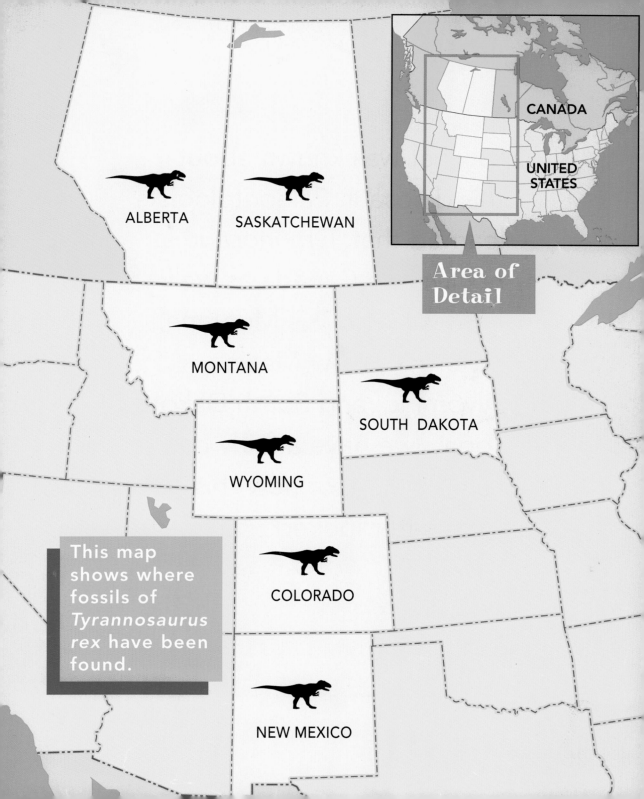

ALBERTA

SASKATCHEWAN

CANADA

UNITED STATES

Area of Detail

MONTANA

SOUTH DAKOTA

WYOMING

This map shows where fossils of *Tyrannosaurus rex* have been found.

COLORADO

NEW MEXICO

to what was known about this dinosaur. Paleontologists learned that *Tyrannosaurus rex* lived in Canada as well as in what now is Montana, Colorado, New Mexico, Wyoming, and South Dakota. Today, we have a fairly complete picture of how this giant flesh eater looked and lived.

King of the Tyrant Lizards

Scientists think that *Tyrannosaurus rex* fully lived up to its name. Like plant-eating dinosaurs, it was often on the move. But unlike the plant eaters, it wasn't looking for green valleys. Instead, it tracked the plant eaters to eat them. It didn't matter that some of these plant-eating dinosaurs were huge. *Tyrannosaurus rex* needed a great deal of meat to survive.

Tyrannosaurus rex tracking a herd of plant-eating dinosaurs

Paleontologists are uncertain about *Tyrannosaurus rex*'s hunting style. It may have scouted a single prey or several prey traveling in a small pack. If it did find a group of horned or duck-billed dinosaurs, it probably didn't attack the whole herd at once. Instead, it probably went after a weak or very young dinosaur. These dinosaurs would have been unlikely to escape or even put up much of a fight.

Some researchers think that *Tyrannosaurus rex* might have relied on both speed and surprise to overcome its prey. It could have waited until a single dinosaur became separated from the herd. Then *Tyrannosaurus rex* might have charged at the animal at a speed of 12 to 20 miles (19 to 32 km) per hour. It would have slammed into its prey with its jaws wide open. This would allow it to quickly sink its teeth into its victim's hide.

At that point, the prey would have no chance of saving itself. Before long, it would be ripped to pieces. If the victim was a small young dinosaur, *Tyrannosaurus rex* might have eaten it in a single bite.

The plant-eating dinosaur *Triceratops* was among the prey of *Tyrannosaurus rex*.

Tyrannosaurus rex attacking a plant-eating dinosaur

Some paleontologists think that *Tyrannosaurus rex* might have been a scavenger as well. This means that it also ate the remains of dinosaurs it found dead in the wild. Those who believe this theory argue that *Tyrannosaurus rex*'s huge bulky body might have made it too slow to easily catch prey. If it wasn't able to surprise its victims, scavenging would have been another way to get food.

Tyrannosaurus rex may have been a scavenger.

The Dinosaur Disappearance

Many people think that all dinosaurs died out at the same time. But it didn't happen quite that way. As a group, dinosaurs existed for about 150 million years. But no one type of dinosaur lasted that long. At various times during the Mesozoic era,

An artist's impression of *Tyrannosaurus rex* seeing a comet head towards Earth

different types of dinosaurs appeared and died out. Most dinosaur species became extinct after only a few million years. Scientists aren't sure why particular dinosaurs died out when they did.

Then, at the end of the Cretaceous period, all the remaining dinosaurs, including *Tyrannosaurus rex*, died out. Even this didn't happen overnight, but over a period of about a million years. No one knows what caused this mass extinction. Many scientists think that it was caused by a specific catastrophe.

One theory is that the dinosaurs became extinct because of the long-term

Many scientists think that the dinosaurs died out because of a "global winter" caused by a comet or asteroid hitting Earth 65 million years ago.

effect of a comet or asteroid crashing into Earth. Comets and asteroids are large bodies that move through space. If a comet or asteroid struck Earth, a tremendous crater would be created. The dust from the hole would float up

Today, fossils are all that are left of dinosaurs.

into the atmosphere. The dust particles would form thick, dark clouds blocking out the Sun. Without sunlight, the weather on Earth would have become quite cold. Some researchers believe dinosaurs could not have survived in such a climate.

Another theory is that environmental change caused the extinction of the dinosaurs. Throughout the Age of the Dinosaurs, the world was changing continually. Large land areas were splitting apart to form continents. Seas and mountain ranges were taking shape as well. As the climate cooled, different types of plant life appeared. Some think that when the dinosaurs could no longer adapt to these global changes, they died out.

Despite some imaginative movie plots, *Tyrannosaurus rex* is not about to return. But we can still learn about this frightening flesh eater from museums and books. And that's about as close as many of us would like to get anyway.

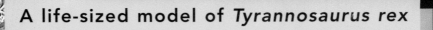

A life-sized model of *Tyrannosaurus rex*

To Find Out More

Here are some additional resources to help you learn more about *Tyrannosaurus rex:*

Books

Aliki. **Fossils Tell of Long Ago.** Crowell, 1990.

Horner, John R. **Digging Up Tyrannosaurus Rex.** Crown, 1992.

Lindsay, William. **Tyrannosaurus.** Dorling Kindersley, 1993.

Most, Bernard. **How Big Were the Dinosaurs?** Harcourt Brace & Co., 1994.

Most, Bernard. **Where to Look for a Dinosaur.** Harcourt Brace Jovanovich, 1993.

Sattler, Helen Roney. **Tyrannosaurus Rex and Its Kin.** Lothrop, Lee & Shephard, 1989.

The Visual Dictionary of Dinosaurs. Dorling Kindersley, 1993.

Organizations and Online Sites

The American Museum of Natural History
Central Park West at
79th Street
New York, NY 10024
http://www. amnh.org

One of the world's largest natural-history museums, it has exceptional collections on dinosaurs and fossils.

Dinorama
http://www. nationalgeographic.com/ dinorama/frame.html

A *National Geographic* site with information about dinosaurs and current methods of learning about them. Includes timelines, animations, and fun facts.

***Tyrannosaurus rex* Page at the Children's Museum of Indianapolis**
http://www. childrensmuseum.org/ dinotrex.htm

A *Tyrannosaurus rex* information page that includes a picture that you can print out and color yourself.

ZoomDinosaurs
http://www. ZoomDinosaurs.com/

Contains everything you might want to know about dinosaurs and other ancient reptiles. Its *Tyrannosaurus* page includes facts, myths, activities, a geologic time chart, print-outs, and links.

Important Words

atmosphere blanket of gases surrounding the Earth

catastrophe great and sudden violent change or disaster

descended developed gradually from over a long period of time

extinct no longer in existence

excavation the process of digging something out

global concerning the entire world

predator animal that preys on other animals

prehistoric existing before humans began recording history through writing

prey animal hunted by another animal

remains bones, teeth, or tissue left behind after a plant or animal dies

serrated toothed or notched like a saw for food

Index

Meet the Author

Elaine Landau has a Bachelor of Arts degree in English and Journalism from New York University and a Master's degree in Library and Information Science from Pratt Institute. She has worked as a newspaper reporter, a children's book editor, and a youth-services librarian, but especially enjoys writing for young people.

Ms. Landau has written more than a hundred nonfiction books on various topics. She lives in Miami, Florida, with her husband, Norman, and son, Michael.

Photographs ©: American Museum of Natural History: 14 (K17403); Ben Klaffke: 15, 18, 20, 23, 24 bottom; Black Hills Institute of Geological Research, Inc.: 21 left, 40; Photo Researchers: 39 (Julian Baum/SPL), 4, 8 (Chris Butler/SPL), 19, 21 right, 24 top, 26, 43 (Francois Gohier), 37 (David A. Hard/SPL), 17 (Jean Philippe/VARIN/JACANA Scientific Control), 10 (Tom McHugh), 2 (David Parker/SPL); The Field Museum, Chicago, IL.: 33 (Painting by Charles Knight/CK9T). Illustrations by Greg Harris